Coffee On Wednesday

By
Charron M. Mollette
Illustrations by Dan Flood

© 2024 Charron M. Mollette

All rights reserved. No part of this book may be used or reproduced by any means, graphic, electronic, or mechanical, including photocopying, recording, taping, or by any information storage retrieval system without written permission of the author except in the case of brief quotations embodied in critical articles and review.

Table of Contents

Dedication
Preface
Introduction

    Ch. 1 - Treehouse
    Ch. 2 - Bus Stop
    Ch. 3 - That "Kat" in the Hat
    Ch. 4 - Mr. Mike
    Ch. 5 - Carriage Ride
    Ch. 6 - Laundry Day
    Ch. 7 - Bartholomew Bucket
    Ch. 8 - Feathers
    Ch. 9 - "Sorry, Wrong Number"
    Ch. 10 - Glass Half Full
    Ch. 11 - Ballet Class
    Ch. 12 - Pillow Talk
    Ch. 13 - Window Seat
    Ch. 14 - Ironing Bored
    Ch. 15 - Buttons
    Ch. 16 - Hot Dog
    Ch. 17 - Circles
    Ch. 18 - The 18th Green
    Ch. 19 - Safe T. Pin
    Ch. 20 - Bikes
    Ch. 21 - Yellow Taxi
    Ch. 22 - Go Fly a Kite
    Ch. 23 - Carrot Top
    Ch. 24 - Square Biz
    Ch. 25 - Wheelbarrow Wisdom
    Ch. 26 - Bananas
    Ch. 27 - Yo-yo
    Ch. 28 - Knock, Knock
    Ch. 29 - The Giraffe Game
    Ch. 30 - Triangle
    Ch. 31 - Red Rose
    Ch. 32 - Crackling Fireplace
    Ch. 33 - Whistle
    Ch. 34 - Motorcycle
    Ch. 35 - "Cosa c'è per cena stasera?" ("What's for dinner tonight?")

Table of Contents
(Continued…)

Ch. 36 - Spiral Staircase
Ch. 37 - Pin Pals
Ch. 38 - Popcorn
Ch. 39 - By Candlelight
Ch. 40 - Boxing Gloves
Ch. 41 - Retired
Ch. 42 - Scary
Ch. 43 - Chair-ished
Ch. 44 - July
Ch. 45 - Sofia
Ch. 46 - A Writer's Recipe
Ch. 47 - Miss Rose A. Parks
Ch. 48 - Ferry Ride
Ch. 49 - Radiohead
Ch. 50 - The "Good-bye" Girl
Ch. 51 - Basket Case
Ch. 52 - Fan Club
Ch. 53 - The "Bourgeois" Belt
Ch. 54 - Captain Cleo Von Kraken
Ch. 55 - Aesthetic
Ch. 56 - Bryson Rashad Nickles

Acknowledgements

Dedication Page

To Auntie Bug (Lawana Rease DeWitty) and cousin Bryson Rashad Nickles

"Auntie Bug is…"

The Alvin Ailey Dance Theater. Judith Jamison performing "Cry"…
"Precious Memories" in church. Stevie Wonder's "Hotter Than July".

"The Graduate" painted by Ernie Barnes. Michael Jackson beats…
"Big Boy Burgers". Cheese Enchiladas. "Famous Amos" cookie treats.

An "Ember" in The Girl Scouts. A Bulldog of Garfield High…
A scarf-wearing Diva. A fashionista who is "Fly".

She's Disneyland, Magic Mountain, and Knott's Berry Farm…
She's the giggling Omega with UCLA charm.

She's Hollywood and Compton. A Student. A Teacher…
A Faithful servant of the Lord, her father was a preacher.

The "Love Ballad" by L.T.D. Songs by Frankie Beverly and MAZE…
The Mademoiselle who started the French beret craze.

The Norman Connor's Starship. The four seasons changing…
watching "The Young and the Restless", as the plots were rearranging.

A Daughter. A Sister. A Mother. A Grandmother…
"Isn't she Lovely?". Unlike no other.

The person I draw my inspiration, because of her loving heart…
The best Auntie I could ever have, our souls will never part.

In memory of: Lawana Rease DeWitty (a.k.a. "Auntie Bug")
For: Charlotte, Rashad, and Bryson Nickles   Love, Charron (*24)

Preface

This book was written to celebrate being your authentic self.

Introduction

Have you ever climbed a treehouse?

"Trees are ever changing like Life."

Chapter 1   "Treehouse"

I'm a kid again, in the branches of an "Oak" tree…
The rustling leaves, the squirrels, and me.

The "Beech" tree heals aches and pains…
It's nature's umbrella when it rains.

The "Maple" is stunning, it has curb appeal…
To deer and elk, they're a big deal.

"Cedar" is sweeter, as an exterior greeter…
For a clubhouse, or a staircase repeater.

Chipmunks and Bears like the "Douglas Fir"…
Dressed in Holiday lights, frankincense, and myrrh.

On a rooftop made of "Pine"…
Birds are chirping, as woodpeckers dine.

From the balcony, a starry night sky…
Where Peter Pan taught Wendy to fly.

An Author's workspace, as she types her next book…
Songwriting a poetic hook.

"Hickory" Barbecue chips, the wood of choice…
A smoky flavor to savor, giving golf balls a voice.

My head is in the clouds, I'm daydreaming of a shed…
Peeking at Robin's eggs, then retiring to bed.

I'm a kid again, in the branches of an "Oak" tree…
The rustling leaves, the squirrels, and me.

Chapter 2   "Bus Stop"

I'm a school bus with no fuss, just fun and folly…
A minivan who can. A jolly trolley.

A multi-passenger vehicle, so commuters can flee…
Escorting, "All-Aboard-ing", for a small fee.

I've been across the country and to Summer Camps…
Met forks in the road, missed "exit" ramps.

I'm a Coach for sightseeing and "away" game trips…
In rainy weather, I slides and I slips.

Uptown, downtown, mid-town, I clown…
Arriving on time, a smile from a frown.

It's truly "the journey", not the destination…
I'm a mini vacation. I'm a "World Tour" location.

In the city looking pretty. An urban legend. A Boss…
Stopping at traffic lights, for people to cross.

On my merry way, staying on a fixed route…
I have snow chains to boot. I successfully scoot.

I'm an "Omnibus", accessible to everyone…
Transporting any pedestrian under the sun.

I'm an articulated accordion, a slinky wiggle wagon…
possessing "Double-decker" charm like a snapdragon.

I'm rapid in transit, navigating streets…
Enjoy riding in comfort, instead of your feets.

My "heels" are wheels, going 'round and 'round…
Towards destiny, adventure, or homeward bound.

Chapter 3   That "Kat" in the Hat

I'm that Victorian Bonnet, worthy of a sonnet…
I'm that carriage-like "calash", with a folded top on it.

In the 1880's, worn by English oarsmen…
I'm that "Straw boater" hat. I'm summer's stand-in.

Gangsters pimpin' Fedoras with "Godfather" swag…
I'm "Indiana Jones". I'm a reason to brag.

Sinatra was handsome in his tilted "Trilby"…
His Seven Hoods were dapper and sharp as could be.

A Beanie would look teeny on the "Cat in the Hat"…
I'm a "Snowmie" in ski gear. I'm chillin'. I'm "Phat".

The two-steppin' Urban Cowboy on the silver screen…
I'm that "Newsboy" or "newsie" headlining the scene.

Je suis ce chapeau de Paris, appelé béret…
Elégante et chic, parce que je suis faite comme ça.

I'm Buster Keaton's "Pork pie", as a bumbling rookie…
or on duty standing watch, wearing a "Snookie".

I'm a Visor, a "Spencer", a sun-blocking wide-brim…
Worn by Clark Gable, "The Panama" loved him.

I'm that felted wool "Top hat", a unique rare find…
I'm that Monopoly game piece, to relax and unwind.

The "Snapback" doesn't slack, nor does the "Pillbox"…
Nor does a nightcap with mis-matching socks.

An Easter bonnet with frills upon it, entering church…
Baseball caps don't take naps, as a thinking perch.

I'm EPMD's "Bucket" hat, giving streetwear its "pop!"…
I'm Run DMC's "Kangol", the "Dope" vibe of Hip-Hop.

Chapter 4   "Mr. Mike"

Energetic excitement, converted by sound…
Reinforcing speech when no one's around.

Microphone check, "One, Two, Three"…
A Comedian's bestie. A Soprano and me.

At school assemblies, I have only one test…
it's to look my best, performing an address.

I'm the audio engineer, songwriting, creating…
A band member in the studio, recording, orchestrating.

I'm that "zing" for hearing a telephone's ring…
I'm quite endearing as Karaoke "bling".

The silent are heard, "Love" is their four-letter word…
I'm absurd as a nerd, imitating a mockingbird.

A "know-it-all" in a concert hall, echoing protocol…
A stinging "Spelling Bee" curveball, for all y'all.

Starring in motion pictures. "Talkies" are my passion…
I wear screenplay dialogue as "literary" fashion.

I'm radio personalities, I'm television broadcasting…
My vibe is a fairytale, happily everlasting.

The spotlight is on me, centerstage is what I like…
How do you do, my name is "Mr. Mike".

Chapter 5   "Carriage Ride"

"Clip-clop, Clip-clop". Cobblestone streets…
Having that "swagger" to "Cuban Cabby" beats.

"Bibbidi, Bobbidi, Boo." At the palace, a rendezvous…
Cinderella was "Fly", then a prince of a guy,
found her glass shoe.

Autumn's harvest. A relaxing Hayride…
Sleigh bells "Jing-a-ling" through the snow as it glides.

For The British Royal Family, "Footmen" are guards…
"Bobbies" uphold the law at Scotland Yard.

It's delivering milk or fish, in a two wheeled cart…
It's Dr. Frankenstein's "hooptie". It's a work of art.

Gladiator Chariots. Coachmen cattle drive…
Chuckwagons fed troops, and helped pioneers survive.

"Clip-clop, Clip-clop". Cobblestone streets…
A horse-drawn carriage, repeating hoofbeats.

Chapter 6   "Laundry Day"

Quarters gobbled up by the washing machine…
Detergent. Fabric Softener. "Fresh". Clean.

Bleaching with delight, for a dinner invite…
Ink is dethroned as a writer's plight.

Coffee, grease, paint, or ketchup stains…
Intensifies an enthusiasm that I can't explains.

The grimiest, The grubbiest, are loads of fun…
After it has spun, the fun has just begun.

An entrancing, enhancing clothesline flow…
Somersaulting in the dryer. All "biz-ness". All Show.

This may portray, or delay, a rhythmic wordplay…
when socks stowaway on laundry day.

Chapter 7   "Bartholomew Bucket"

Wood, plastic, or metal, a flat bottom container…
A bubbling kettle. From a well,
a complainer.

Capturing the flow of a leaky ceiling show…
Candles low in a row, shoveling snow.

I adore mopping floors and other chores…
detailing vehicles and just being outdoors.

Kettles of fish, pitchers of punch…
Jugs of lemonade and apple cider with lunch.

A pail has a lid, I however, do not…
I'm a makeup caddie, mixing paint on the spot.

I'm a car, called a "Hooptie", poppin' bubble gum…
I'm a musical instrument. A mathematical sum.

I hold dollar bills, in the money game…
If I had a hole, that would be a shame.

Chapter 8   "Feathers"

In poetry, in paintings, light as air, flying free…
Guidance through wisdom, the **Black** feathers of me.

Giving pillows their "puffy-ness", brightening up a room…
Performing in the "Cabaret" in an ostrich costume.

Calming relaxation, the energy of **Blue**…
a crown of **Brown**, with reconnecting to do.

A Peacock's tail. Eagles in flight…
A masquerade party at the stroke of midnight.

Happiness is great when **Green** is on the scene…
Orange is inspiring, creative, pristine.

Earrings that dangle like ornamental flowers…
Pausing for a moment or meditating for hours.

Pink means that Love knows no bounds…
The power of **Red** is as strong as it sounds.

Forrest Gump was an extraordinary guy…
His dream was a wish to the stars in the sky.

Yellow is cheerful, just as it seems…
Pursue your desire. Focus on your dreams.

A feathered fan compliments a wide-brim summer hat…
A feather boa in da' Club is "Phat" and "All That".

I'm Divine protection when Angels are around…
Peaceful Positivity when a **White** feather is found.

In poetry, in paintings, light as air, flying free…
Guidance through wisdom are the feathers of me.

Chapter 9   "Sorry, Wrong Number"

Edison's invention, an innovative intention…
Communication has expanded beyond comprehension.

"Give me them digits, what's your phone number?
I plan on waking you from a sound slumber."

A phone booth, a phone book, White or Yellow pages…
Phonetically, alphabetically, in various stages.

If lines were busy on a rotary phone…
Someone will assist you, so you're never alone.

If you get disconnected, an operator connects you…
Tracing calls are done by a selected few.

A landline is not needed for a cellular device…
An apparatus transmitting sound is pretty nice.

Answering machines are trustworthy, with the data they keep…
Please leave a message after the ("Beep!").

A unique ring tone can buzz just because…
Long distance transmission is easier than it was.

Dialing "M" was the plot for Alfred Hitchcock's thriller…
Barbara Stanwyck heard the footsteps of her killer.

"Nickel-plated desktop", or "Candlestick" style…
The oilcan base and tapered shaft can beguile.

General Electric's "Potbelly". The "push button" evolves…
"Ma Bell" loves web browsing and the problems it solves.

Edison's invention, an innovative intention…
Communication has expanded beyond comprehension.

Chapter 10   "Glass Half Full"

I'm a "Back-in-the-day-Kool-Aid-drinking" kid…
Ice water and Sweet Tea are where ice cubes stay hid.

With a paper umbrella as my chapeau…
J'adore tropical getaways, ya' know.

Hosting celebrity roasts, giving a champagne toast…
Hot cocoa is what marshmallows "dig" the most.

I'm New Year's cheer. I'm pints of beer…
I'm wine. I'm divine, it's obviously clear.

"Dear Santa" letters. Milk and cookies, a fireplace…
Naughty and Nice. Blessings and Grace.

A Tea kettle's whistle, flirting with steam…
A muffin's true love? A cup of tea with cream.

Coffee on Tuesdays, a sunshining reign…
Reading Ichabod Crane, to "bookishly" ascertain.

Orange juice to "Get Well". Ginger Ale cold as ice…
Pineapple soda is refreshingly nice.

I'm a "Back-in-the-day-Kool-Aid-drinking" kid…
Ice water, Sweet Tea, ice cubes stay hid.

Chapter 11 "Ballet Class"

Backstage was Edgar Degas, capturing power and grace…
Oil painted dancers in their practicing space.

The charming Mademoiselle De Lafontaine…
On the Opera stage, triumphant to entertain.

A grand jeté by Pavlova making a lasting impression…
Fairytales and fantasy with artistic expression.

Prima Ballerina, Janet Collins performing at "The Met"…
A Raven Wilkinson relevé or prestigious pirouette.

Thunderous applause for "The Red Shoes" in 5th position…
"The Nutcracker" captivates even during intermission.

The movement "pas de deux" means "step of two"…
Leslie Caron did a duet in her motion picture debut.

The Alvin Ailey Dance Theater is fluidity in motion…
The New York City Ballet, a dance company with devotion.

Misty Copeland held her arms in "Arabesque" style…
Her grand plié, as Tchaikovsky's swan, was done with a smile.

Flutes, Piccolos, Violins, Brass instruments, and Percussion…
Clarinets, Double basses, and Harps, harmonized in discussion.

The Dance Theater of Harlem, empowerment illumes…
Magical, mythical characters "make-believe" in costumes.

The elegance of Adagio, it's an illusion most master…
The beauty of Allegro, its movements are faster.

It's "Giselle", "The Firebirds", "A Midsummer Night's Dream"…
It's "Don Quixote", "Coppélia", expressing poetic themes.

Fairytales and fantasy. Storytelling comes to pass…
as Tutus and black leotards are worn in ballet class.

Chapter 12   "Pillow Talk"

Fluffy. Puffy. Feather or down…
I'm Memory foam. Amnesia, my crown.

The Buckwheat. The Beanbag. Silently snoring…
Counting sheeps with my "Peeps" isn't boring.

Pajamas and slippers. Footies for feets…
Getting comfy on a mattress with brand new sheets.

A Bedtime story written in my head…
Thankful for blessings before going to bed.

A Twin, a Full, a Queen, a King…
It's both a "day and nighttime" thing.

Looking "Fly", don't know why, in my bonnet nightcap…
On the sofa, or a rug, for an afternoon nap.

A dwarf named "Sleepy" had six other roommates…
Befriending "Snow White". Off to work, never late.

One pillow, two pillows, three, four, or five…
for a dorm room, an office, any decorating Jive.

Doris Day and Rock Hudson delighted the silver screen…
Falling in love, pillow-talking each scene.

Fluffy and Puffy for a good night…
Cradling her dreams as she continues to write.

Chapter 13   "Window Seat"

Gazing in amazement, through the window I see…
infinite rainbows smiling back at me.

Catching sight of pinecones hitting the ground…
Do they say "Ouch!" when no one's around?

Hitchcock gave a glimpse through a neighbor's eyes…
As an amateur sleuth solves a mystery he spies.

Peering through the porthole of prosperity and Peace…
Possibly peek-a-booing with peeping expertise.

Beyond the night sky with cosmic delight…
Envisioning wishes, stars twinkling bright.

Snow-dancing and prancing, enhances romancing…
Glancing at circumstances are entrancing.

Ostentatious jewelry. Diamonds being blunt…
Admiring "bling" displayed in a storefront.

Gawking at the beauty of gorgeous stained-glass…
With flecks of "fabulous" surpassing upper-class.

Curtains and shutters, a panoramic view…
Observing and studying vertical blinds too.

Self-reflection revealing images of the past…
Windows of opportunity, making memories last.

Gazing in amazement, through the window I see…
infinite rainbows smiling back at me.

Chapter 14 "Ironing Bored"

Controlling the temperature for cotton and lace…
Silk, wool, and satin. A polyester pace.

Starting with the sleeves when starching shirts…
Moving on to the collar. With neckties, I flirts.

Linen fabric is chosen, again and again…
Equestrienne fashion or a fancy napkin.

My performance is neat. I aim to please…
Putting creases in blue jeans or trousers with ease.

I'm the "pro" in Professional and formal occasions…
For newspaper printing with pressing persuasion.

I'm Superfly like "Shaft", always dressed to impress…
Appeared on "The Late Show", adding "swag" to a dress.

I'm steaming toward a storyboard award…
Un-crinkling wrinkles with a coiled cord.

Chapter 15   "Buttons"

We're sewn onto garments, fastening fronts…
We're impressive operators. We do our own stunts.

With needle and thread, clothing is our best friend…
We're a badge designed with a slogan then pinned.

We're exactly right. We're always on time…
Technical yet timid, the key to this rhyme.

"Cute" and astute, we compliment leather boots…
It's hard to compute why we're so absolute.

We're rivets in jeans, sturdy and strong…
A handed-down wedding gown, or a sarong.

Shirts and sweaters together, in cooler seasons…
Marching band uniforms, for obvious reasons.

A fitted blazer, silk scarf, or tailored pants…
At the dry cleaners, the seamstress will enhance.

We're "do-it-yourself". We're collected in a mug…
We're a Teddy bear's eyes when it's time to hug.

We're "Polyester Jesters", fantastic, made of plastic…
A glass 'hood. Tufting wood. Enthusiastic.

We're "seashell" clientele, where oysters dwell…
Stone, metal, and coconut are also quite swell.

We snap faster than the cuff links, adorning the arm…
We're toggles, we're "studs" with magnetic charm.

Chapter 16   "Hot Dog"

Just call me "Frank". I love summertime…
With my "grill-friends". I'm the Hot "dawg" of this rhyme.

Flustered with mustard at the State Fair…
Ketchup, relish, and onions were there.

I'm silly with chili, at the beach or at home…
I'm family and liked wherever I roam.

A magic trick on a stick, in a cornmeal disguise…
My craving companions? A side of French fries.

"Hamburger Homies" tango with potato salad…
I'm the lyrics when grilling in a camping ballad.

A European dish, with a Vienna voice...
Aerodynamic. A Sauerkraut choice.

I'm "Nathan" from Coney Island. I'm "Street cuisine"…
I'm a "weenie" named "Oscar" at a baseball scene.

Made from beef, turkey, chicken, or pork…
Some eat Vegan. Some dine with a fork.

Am I a sandwich? Yes, some would agree…
Let me be "frank", you'll fall in love with me.

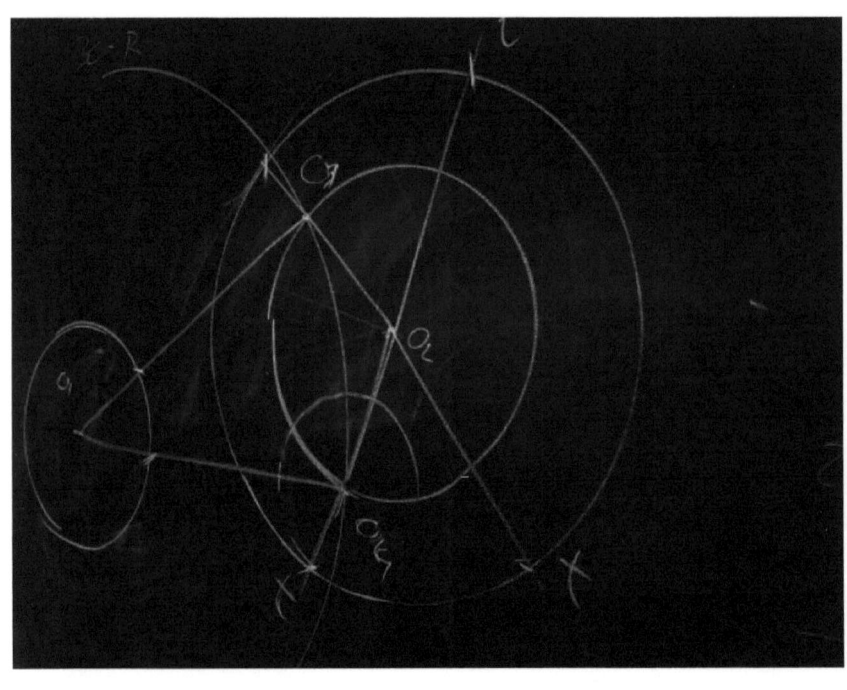

Chapter 17   "Circles"

We're amusement park rides, in a revolving motion…
Delicious flat breads. A cauldron potion.

We're rims on a "Hooptie", golf balls on the green...
45-inch records I bought as a teen.

There's a rumor on Mars about the Moon…
and other planets in the galaxy, resembling balloons.

We're the circumference of a soccer or bowling ball…
Properties of math, great and small.

We're pocket watches, ticking and telling time…
We're the eyes of the Tiger, platinum records of rhymes.

We're Birthday cakes, a camera lens…
Olympic medals, where everyone wins.

We're ornaments for Christmas, or earring hoops…
Bowls of cereal, hot homemade soups.

We're a giant Lollipop, not a candy cane…
The direction of propellers on an airplane.

We're traffic lights, the slow of yellow…
In the word "zero". Poetically mellow.

We're sand dollars found walking on the beach…
Diamonds, sweet peas, pies made of peach.

We're buttons on sweaters, blouses, and shirts…
Fried onion rings, ambivert experts.

We're a trampoline, bellyflopping at times…
Pennies, nickels, quarters, and dimes.

We're peanut butter cookies with chocolate chips…
Jewelry like pearls. Hula-hooping backflips.

We're donuts and bagels, or figure eights…
We're family and friends. It's "Love" we create.

Chapter 18   "The 18th Green"

He's Gifted. He's Golf Clubs. This Tiger wears the Crown…
He's Peete, Elder, and Sifford. He's Dewey Brown.

A Green Jacket Gamer. No Time for Drama...
Got his Skillz from his Pops. Got his Smile from his Mamma.

He's Precise, Triple Nice, Kindness Multiplied Twice…
He's Fairways and Eagles. His Backhand is like Ice.

Knock, Knock. Who's There? The "Kat" whose got Swag…
The Birdie Master in Lay-Up Freeze Tag.

He hits gentle Fades, from the Tee with bliss…
Others shanking, Airmailing into the Abyss.

He's Backspin Bluegrass. The Chip Shot is his Throne…
He Strikes. He Doubles. He Gobbles and Hambones.

The Gallery hushes, then the Dimples are hit…
His Barkies are Ballets, even Caddies yell, "Sit!".

The St. Andrews Ace. Just a "Kidd" with a jug…
He's Legendary as The Open. A Driving Jitterbug.

May the "fore" be with him as he Goes Low on the Scene…
Finishing with Finesse on the 18th Green.

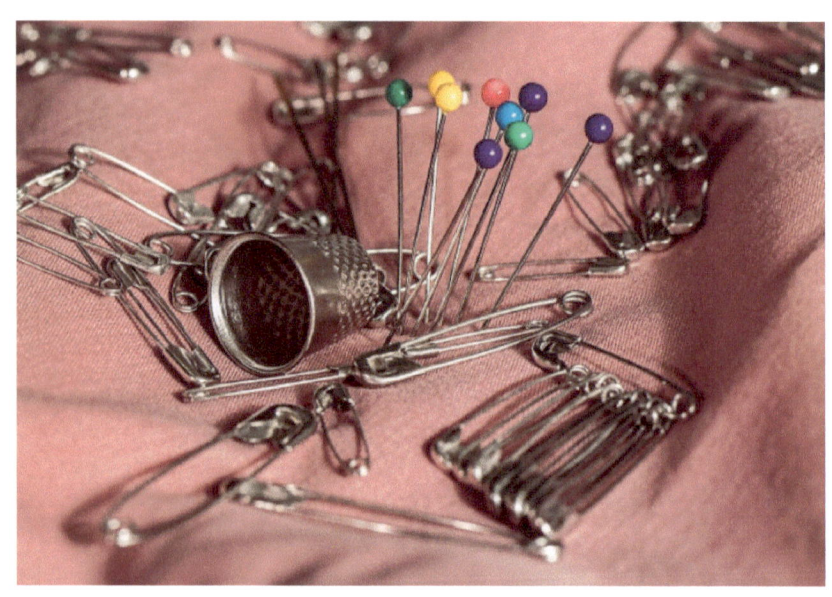

Chapter 19   "Safe T. Pin"

I'm sure and secure. Cinching and clinching…
"Bossing" and broaching. Punk-rocking. Three-inching.

Fastening dresses and cloaks, holding togas in place…
A kilt piercing style, pointing towards grace.

Buckling. Chuckling. Catching and patching…
Clamping on clothing. Attention snatching.

Solidarity. Rebellion. New ways to live…
I'm listening. I'm here, with "Love" to give.

Chapter 20   "Bikes"

I had a red tricycle when I was a tyke…
I named her "Lucille". She had "swag". My first bike.

On my 6th birthday, a banana seat, yellow "Schwinn"…
Got a blue 10-speed when I was 10.

I met "Low Riders" during summer visits to "Cali"…
Compton, Beverly Hills, and "homies" from "the valley".

In a rodeo, in the mountains, or off-road dirt trails…
Navigating suspension, telling rigid tales.

Saw a "Boss" of motocross. In muddy waters, precocious…
A BMX daredevil whose middle name is "Ferocious".

Trudged up and down hills, with a Hybrid and helmet…
Did stationary workouts to stay physically fit.

Had a "Tandem" built for two, but on a different path…
Learned to unicycle and I did my own math.

Cruising, miles to go in an upright position…
Dreaming of a journey, my heart's intuition.

Reclining and coasting on a "Recumbent" Bike…
complements my silver hair, which is what I like.

Chapter 21   "Yellow Taxi"

I have a checkerboard trim, I'm part of a fleet…
Drivers in the front, "players" in the backseat.

En route to the airport for an early flight…
The fare is metered, day or night.

Scorsese's "Taxi Driver" is on the verge of obsession…
A film where DeNiro narrates a loneliness confession.

On a backroad not taken, sliding Uptown to hide…
Am I coming and going? Or just along for the ride?

To a curbside car wash, near the sidewalk…
A destination dispatcher. Heavy traffic talk.

Known for life lessons and its opening theme…
A sitcom about cabbies trying to fulfill their dream.

I take comfort in knowing the joy of puddle playing…
I'm not staying, I must finish highway-ing.

I have a checkerboard trim, I'm part of a fleet…
Drivers in the front, "players" in the backseat.

Chapter 22 "Go Fly a Kite"

On a clear day, I am free…
marveling at the things I see.

There are clouds, and trees, and bugs, and birds…
Was that a helicopter I just heards?

My colorful personality is my long tail…
It's part of my charm, as a boat with a sail.

With gusts of wind, my dance begins…
Flirting with the breeze, where we both wins.

Climbing and maintaining my altitude…
Twirling and swirling if I'm in the mood.

Is this what it feels like to be a butterfly?
Suddenly transformed, becoming one with the sky.

On a clear day, I am free…
I was high as a kite,
now I'm stuck in a tree.

Chapter 23   "Carrot Top"

I grew up in a garden,
the country life is charming…
I have cabbage and turnip cousins,
rooted in farming.

I know a rabbit named "Harvey",
and a bunny called "Bugs"…
And **a red-haired comedian**,
who spreads laughter like hugs.

Springtime with my "homies",
painted eggs are "dandy"…
I'm a measurement, spelled differently,
I'm *Diamond* eye candy.

I'm freshly tossed into salads,
in a mélange of players…
In pots of comfort food,
majestic **cakes** with three layers.

I improve eyesight with **Vitamin "see"**…
What's a snowman without me?
No one **nose** but he.

Chapter 24   "Square Biz"

I'm twice as nice as sugar and spice…
A gift to "High rollers" as "Lady Luck" holds the dice.

Joyful. "Toy-ful". A Jack-in-the-box…
I'm a neighborhood composed of several blocks.

An Einstein of design, four sides is my shrine…
Checkerboard players think I'm divine.

Twisting and turning a "Rubik's Cube" puzzle…
I'm the texture of waffles, with syrup to nuzzle.

I'm "Sponge Bob's" pants for underwater dancing…
"Teena Marie" and her "biz" were "Hip-Hop" enhancing.

I'm the interior motif of ultramodern smiles…
I'm sophisticated ceramic floor tiles.

Paper napkins at parties, celebrations begin…
Not tangled, right-angled, reflecting my twin.

I'm quadrilateral, my sides the same length…
Some say I'm old-fashioned, with inner strength.

A Graham cracker or Saltine. A grid-like landscape…
I'm an ice cubist and "square" is my shape.

Chapter 25   "Wheelbarrow Wisdom"

I haul stuff around. I can handle the job…
In pumpkin patches. In a gardening mob.

One sturdy wheel, that's how I roll…
I'm a mobile buddy. I'm a funny shaped bowl.

Plants and mulch. Trash and tools…
'round the clock, moving rocks, breaking no rules.

I made a wish; my wish came to me…
To carry soil, mulch, and gravel for free.

At construction sites mixing concrete…
Gliding across grass, just like bare feet.

Loading a station wagon with the full moon…
in a cleverly animated, creative "cart-toon".

I can handle the job. I haul stuff around…
I'm a workaholic. My purpose, I've found.

Chapter 26   "Bananas"

I'm a "Pimp" in pancakes, breakfast, or brunch…
Made hot and cold cereals trendy for lunch.

I'm "Bake sale" muffins. I go "nutty" with bread…
Have attended receptions after couples were wed.

More than a Smoothie, I'm a "flavor earthquake"…
A tropical drink. A soda fountain milkshake.

Not to brag or boast, but I'm fluent in "French toast"…
With Amaretto ice cream I'm definitely "the most".

Made famous as Elvis' "Peanut butter" sandwich…
I'm a fritter, Pudding-sitter. Desserts, I enrich.

I'm a "Hummingbird" Cake, made with loving hands...
I'm the costumed characters of "The Banana Splits" band.

Some call me "Foster", I'm a southern dish…
Butter. Brown Sugar. Rum sauce. Delish.

I'm cupcakes, Bundt cakes, a nutritious treat…
A star in fruit salads and delicious to eat.

Chapter 27   "Yo-yo"

A toy on a string, spun up and down…
A "rapper" from Compton with her empowerment crown.

"Pinwheel" momentum as it unwinds…
It's "Double or Nothing". It can't be confined.

A "Breakaway" attitude from a "Basic throw"…
You're on your own when "Lindy Looping" ya' know.

An Upper or Lower "Finger spin Curl"…
Tricky angle rotations, "Barrel rolling" a twirl.

"Splitting the Atom" isn't just scientific…
It's a flick of the wrist to be more specific.

For "Brain twisting" beginners, or slackers "Shock waving"…
(*"Boing!"*) is the sound when it's misbehaving.

Flipping and zipping on its trapeze…
Rounded in shape, "butterfly-ing" with ease.

Ingenuity and velocity spinning up and down…
Gravity defines this free-falling noun.

Chapter 28   "Knock, Knock"

At the A.M. of Four, there was a knock at my door…
Waking me as I snored, I heard knocking twice more.

Could it be the Bad Wolf from "The Three Little Pigs"?
or the one from "Red Riding Hood" with grandma's wig?

Maybe it's opportunity or Jacob Marley's ghost…
Is it the Academy Awards members wanting me as the host?

What if it's someone who's lost their way…
maybe it's a movie star needing somewhere to stay.

Sleepwalking down the stairs, only wearing one slipper…
Throwing on my "Elvis" robe, fuddling with the zipper.

Are Zombies attacking? Am I in danger?
Is this a chance meeting for me and a stranger?

Down the hallway I went, through the living room…
passed the hall closet where I keep the broom.

Will it be Michael Myers standing in the doorway…
wearing a bedsheet with nothing to say?

Are "The Doors" at my door igniting a trend?
The problem with their songs is that they end.

The knocking loosened hinges and shook the frame…
From struggles to blessings, to a destined fame.

On the threshold of unlocking episodes of wonder…
Welcoming peace of mind as it sleeps in thunder.

Tomorrows look like yesterdays, it's not hard to tell…
The hinges moved from their groove, in tandem with the doorbell.

A "door" is not just an object that is latched…
It possesses Architectural Spirit that's unmatched.

I'm living the dream of where I want to be…
Faithfully walking through the doors, that are in front of me.

Chapter 29   "The Giraffe Game"

We browse on twigs, grass, and shrubs…
We're long-lasting cliques. We form our own clubs.

We grunt and hum, mindful to what's around…
Snorting and hissing, with flute-like sounds.

Vigilantes standing strong, tall, and lean…
our gangly legs running, a sleek machine.

We're cuter than a stuffed animal toy…
Stepped onto Noah's Ark with Faith and Joy.

We're thoroughly convinced and not conceded…
Graceful in stature. We're muses repeated.

A spotted complexion. Self-expressive fame…
We journey with discovery in "The Giraffe Game".

Chapter 30 "Triangle"

A journey to the monumental Egyptian Pyramids…
A pool shark, the "Hustler", that "Fast Eddie" kid.

Mountain peaks capped with snow touching the sky…
The number "4" has a triangle like a quarter of pie.

Hangers in the closet are hardly ever alone…
An object to warn drivers are bright plastic cones.

A banner or flag waving in the air…
A stylish bandana or silk scarf headwear.

Sailing in Bermuda, a fathom depth is six feet…
A percussion instrument for calling loved ones to eat.

Similar in shape, the letters "A" and "V"…
Mathematically triangular. A "3-sided" spelling bee.

Watermelon wedges. Candy corn. A Witch's Hat…
A camping tent, there's no better shelter than that.

Dressed to impress, I'm right-angle obsessed…
Faithfully guided, I'm Truly Blessed.

Chapter 31   "Red Rose"

Without words, I'm stunning as a bouquet…
Long, poetic stems on Valentine's Day.

The epitome of beauty, a handsome "Chick"…
A gardening expression, a shade of lipstick.

A perennial shrub, thorny, prickly…
A scientific serenade, with a scent that's tickle-ly.

Delicate petals, making bumblebees blush…
Rose hips in tea, Van Gogh's paintbrush.

Sung by Bette Midler, composed by McBroom…
I symbolize "love" in full bloom.

A rose, I suppose, by any other name…
still smells sweet, Shakespeare said the same.

Whispering memories, thoughts of the past…
The stronger the roots, the longer I last.

Floral foliage, its fragrance fantastic…
Imitations are made from recycled plastic.

Without words, I'm stunning as a bouquet…
My long, poetic stems bring hope for today.

Chapter 32   "Crackling Fireplace"

Holiday stockings and garland, I'm built for "snuggle" weather…
Tranquility and I somehow go together.

I'm an artist's creation, a masterpiece made of ice…
I'm in a log cabin, roasting marshmallows twice.

After smoke billows up, down comes Saint Nick…
Sweepers, hearth keepers, cleaning chimneys quick.

Blowing bursts of air increasing the flame…
The passageway is called a "flue", its formal name.

A rectangular opening helping fires burn bright…
Vigil fires are reminiscent of a wintery night.

To protect from embers, some wear caps on their head…
A fashion statement when you're ready for bed.

I'm fire logs burning or electric and sleek…
Without emitting soot, some are "gas" furnace geeks.

I'm a double-sided centerpiece dividing a room…
An interior design kept tidy with a broom.

A pot full of beans, brushing clean on the scene…
"Three-point" cooking with a decorative screen.

The "Dope" style of tile and marble stones…
Brick is the backdrop of scented pinecones.

For moving ashes and coals, my "Bestie" is a "spade"…
Tongs shifting logs as if they got paid.

Pushing and pulling logs, like a practical joker…
Without risking injury, it's the job of a "poker".

I'm Zen with grace in a heated space…
Artwork sits on my mantel, I'm a crackling fireplace.

Chapter 33 "Whistle"

The "5 o'clock whistle" didn't blow…
"Ella Fitzgerald" sang about it, wouldn't ya' know.

The "chugging" train, forlorn in the night…
Brakes "hissing" and "screeching" with delight.

Referees ensure the rules of fair play…
maintaining sportsmanship in a safe way.

I'm a teakettle made from stainless steel metal…
Whistling a happy tune for sellers who peddle.

The "*whizzing*" wind "***whooshing***" with eerie pitching…
Twitching, snitching, forever bewitching.

I train dogs when they scurry, so don't worry…
I'm "Whistler's Mother". Iconic, not blurry.

Meadowlarks and sparrows are music to the ear…
Their spoken words quoting William Shakespeare.

I was rhyming in rhythm, alongside my crew…
And kept rhyming, after the "5 o'clock whistle" blew.

Chapter 34   "Old Lady Ludwig"

I'm that "**Harley-Davidson**", "**BMW**", or "**Ducati**"…
I'm "The Leader of the Pack", like a "**Maserati**".

Eric Von Zipper is a "Homie" of mine…
Met "**The Doctor**", a "**Grand Prix**" winner times nine.

I'm for "**Sliders**", "**Easy Riders**", I'm a '52 "hog"…
A stars-and-stripes painted fuel tank, for a "**Badd Dog**".

I'm a "**Joker**", a "**Jet**", doing roadster things…
I'm a grizzly "**Bear**" of a bike, a "**Honda**" with wings.

A "**Drifter**" who's swifter than a "**Ninja**" doing tricks…
"Not all who wander are lost.", just cruising for kicks.

I'm that "**Yamaha**", "**Suzuki**", or "**Ducati**"…
I'm "The Leader of the Pack", like a "**Maserati**".

Chapter 35　　"Cosa c'è per cena stasera?"
　　　　　　　("What's for dinner tonight?")

Un delizioso pasto a base di noodles e salsa…
Un padrino, un bravo ragazzo, un boss della pasta.

Salsiccia, polpette, and maiale in mamma's recipe…
Aggiungere un po' di zucchero, questa è la chiave.

Spaghetti is plural for *spaghetto*, a thin string or twine…
With family and friends, with bottles of wine.

Per una signora e un vagabondo, una bella notte…
Sharing a "Tony's Special" plate, a kiss by moonlight.

"Throwing Spaghetti", it'll stick if it can…
It's trying an idea without a plan.

Basilico, origano, flavors and seasonings…
A garden of veggies and olive reasonings.

Pane all'aglio e lume di candela…
Ehi, cosa c'è per cena stasera?

Chapter 36   "Spiral Staircase"

Disappearing in pages without a trace…
A beanstalk among books, a writing space.

Some linger, some learn, some snooze and such…
Some rehearsing "Hamlet", protesting too much.

I'm helix-shaped, like the "Miraculous Stair"…
Southwestern woodwork with remarkable flair.

I'm an ice-skater's axel jump frozen in time…
I'm a scientific shape, twirling my rhyme.

Hibernating in the halls of a library or home…
A writer's imagination is where I love to roam.

I'm a story transporter, skipping steps makes me shorter…
Ascending and descending in alphabetical order.

Disappearing in pages without a trace…
A beanstalk among books, a writing space.

Chapter 37   "Pin Pals"

I'll try and spare you from the bowling puns…
But you might frame the "punny" ones.

I'm an Alley "Kat", a "pocket" roller…
When I play in the morning, I'm a "cereal" bowler.

One ball, One lane, against Ten pins…
Let the good times bowl, the top score wins.

A string of six strikes is called "a sixer"…
Non-sliding shoes is an ideal elixir.

Met "The Bowling Stones" they're Too Legit to Split…
It would be "gutter-ly" ridiculous if they quit.

For lane approaches, patrons are "Pin" pals…
like the Flintstone and Rubble guys and gals.

Split happens. Split ends. New Skids on the Block…
That Big Lebowski "dude" and his team really "Rock".

Twelve strikes are non-existent, like the "dinosaur"…
A "Three Hundred" game on a shiny, wood floor.

I tried to spare you from the bowling puns…
But you may have to frame the "punny" ones.

Chapter 38 "Popcorn"

I'm heated seeds of corn, that burst with a ("*pop!*")...
"A-maize-ingly" adored, from a family-owned crop.

Snackable, Sack-a-ble, more than 5,000 years old...
In movie theaters, I'm buckets of gold.

I'm simply scrumptious, can't be overpowered...
For circusgoers, I'm deliciously devoured.

I'm from a corn cob. I hob nob, it's my job...
I'm salted and buttered for a hungry mob.

Sometimes I'm mushroom-shaped,
sometimes I'm Butterfly...
Irregular indeed, without having to try.

I'm television's "Bestie" for the "Superbowl"...
Sprinkled with cheddar cheese, with a caramelized soul.

I'm a ball of fun. "Trick or Treaters", I spoil...
I have the remarkable aroma of coconut oil.

Let me husk you a question: Do you like "Cracker Jacks"?
Prefer "Kettle Corn" or flaming hot snacks?

Crunchy for "the munchies". Fluffy and scruffy...
I'm a "Phat Kat", who loves being puffy.

I'm heated seeds of corn, that burst with a ("*pop!*")...
"A-maize-ingly" adored, from a family-owned crop.

Chapter 39   "By Candlelight"

In the coziness of the couch, cuddled with insight...
writing "punny" poetry, fading into the night.

Inspiration is nimble, my pen is quick...
creating "shtick" as quick as Saint Nick.

The solace, the silence, the whisper of flames...
flickering, frolicking, to its own name.

Jazzy, snazzy, made from Beeswax...
Duke Ellington's band, a soloist on the sax.

Shy, but "Fly". Vanilla soy can be coy...
Illuminating joy like a Holiday toy.

Spiritual truth. Faithful celebrations...
like Fireflies in a jar, giving good vibrations.

Seeing through the darkness with ease is a breeze...
Healing from within by praying on my knees.

Fragrant motives of votives, hope and gratitude...
some are spellbinding, some remind me of food.

"The Memoirs of Casanova", Candelabras, applause...
A "Liberace" concerto performed just because.

On a Book Club train trip, a romance began...
Engaging readers with words is the author's plan.

It's spirits from the past, a "haunted house" thing...
Its sparkling "bling" making hearts sing.

My enchanting night, greeted dawn's light...
Candles burning bright, as I continue to write.

Chapter 40   "Boxing Gloves"

Jack Johnson broke barriers with his defense…
Known as the "Galveston Giant", his gameplan was intense.

A trip to the canvas, "Fisticuffs" combat…
"The Greatest" was Ali, as Liston hit the mat.

Running, punching bags, and jumping rope…
"Duck and Draw", "*Bob and Weave*", and "Rope-a-Dope".

"Toe-to-Toe" is the show amongst defenders…
for prizefighter Joe Louis and fringe contenders.

Somebody up there likes "The Italian Stallion"…
Wearing "The Championship Belt" like a medallion.

Robinson and Leonard, both named "Sugar Ray"…
Technical Knockouts, deserve a replay.

Mike Tyson wears a mouthpiece playing "Peek-A-Boo"…
Mayweather Jr. has some "south-pawing" to do.

Foreman, Frazier, and Holyfield, legendary Heavyweights…
Two who share gym training are called "Stablemates".

The "Shoeshine" method, the flashy punches are quick…
Leaving a lasting impression, that may do the trick.

A challenger in a 'Bout, crossing with the right…
Mastering footwork in a Welter-weight fight.

An effective offense with blows to the gut…
then a hook combination, with a quick uppercut.

Sticking and *moving*. Jabbing glass jaws…
"The Main Event" fight of gifted paws.

From a neutral corner, for 12 rounds in the ring…
Shadow boxing, until the bell goes ("*Ding!*")

Chapter 41 "Retired"

Was a "Boss" on the road, at the Drive-in on a date…
I believe early is on time, and on time is late.

Leading lakeside caravans of family and friends…
Hauling lumber with snow chains amidst howling winds.

A car show favorite, trophies cram the bookshelf…
Became an Old School success despite myself.

I have a master's degree in pneumatics and Liberal Arts…
I'm the King of cargo, towing book smarts.

My dress code is comfort, love denim overalls…
Work best after oil changes and tune-ups when I crawls.

My body is rusty, I get "geezer" mail…
I'm American graffiti, off the sunset trail.

Chapter 42   "Scary"

A sinister story of howling winds…
As this shocking "Thriller" of a rhyme begins.

The infamous shower scene at the "Bates Motel"…
If you *scream* in outer space, there's no one to tell.

The "Rear Window" sill. "The Birds" did follow…
The legendary tale of "Sleepy Hollow".

A little "Hocus-Pocus" at "The Monster Mash"…
Mummies wrapped in linen sheets, like an endless sash.

Count Orlok's Castle is a Transylvanian fright…
At the Opera, on "The Phantom's" opening night.

Near Amity Island there swam a big fish…
It terrorized a small town. It was Nightmare-ish.

Creatures hunting by sound in a Zombie land…
During "Twilight" a romance began.

On Friday the 13th at Camp Crystal Lake…
Under the full moon Jason's mother was awake.

"The Addams Family". Frankenstein and his bride…
Boris Karloff gave *fear* nowhere to hide.

John Carpenter's famous scene in "Halloween"…
"The Boogie Man" comes home on the silver screen.

Wanna see something scary? I'll bet you do…
"Boo."

Chapter 43   "Chair-ished"

My simplistic design is nerdy, yet sturdy…
With folding card tables, I tend to be flirty.

I'm a place to read the morning paper, by a roaring fire…
Or the literary journal, by Sir John Collings Squire.

I'm a vintage "knick-knack" for a welcoming guest…
Like a handmade quilt on a rocker's armrest.

I'm Elizabethan on stage, a Windsor by name…
I'm Louis XVI elegance, in a musical party game.

I have Rustic diversity, a Rosewood smile…
Loved for my knowledge of Victorian style.

Wrought Iron or Rosewood. Ornate or plain…
I'm a wicker patio set, left outside in the rain.

In a Gothic palace. In a Snowmie's Igloo…
Gilligan's fun-niture was made from Bamboo.

Laid-back and groovy, the Bean bag is "far out!"…
It's got clout, no doubt. Other chairs pout.

As a playwright's page is rehearsed on stage…
My loose joints are restored, concealing my age.

I have a confession, a designing obsession…
Italian Renaissance is my form of expression.

My twin cousins are recliners, "The Lazy Boyz"…
We've been to Santa's Workshop, watched elves make toys.

At the Paris "Cabaret" as I perform…
The "Flashdance" and me create the perfect storm.

Met the "Fresh" prince of Bel-chair, a jewel of a stool…
with the gift to uplift. In two words, "really Kool".

I'm a Chair-ished antique. I'm old and new…
A blessed collectible. Faithful as a church pew.

Chapter 44   "July"

Independence. Freedom. Family. Barbeques…
At the beach. At the park. Soft drinks and booze.

It's hotter than July or a Jalapeño's armpit…
Spent a "Stevie Wonder" summer rappin' about it.

Burgers, chips, and dip. Hot dogs. Potato salad…
Traffic taillights composing honking ballad.

Underneath the stars, singing campfire songs…
Cruisin' by the lakeside all night long.

Pyro technicians. Fireworks zoom…
LOUD whistling and then, ("Snap! *Crackle!* **Boom***!*").

Bursts of colors flashing in the evening sky…
A nightery of excite-tery on the Fourth of July.

Chapter 45   "Sofia"

Relax in the living room, while I describe…
my "Chesterfield" pedigree and French Vanilla vibe.

Pile on the pillows, throw blankets on me…
I've administered meetings as an employee.

The television and I are the best of friends…
Hosting old movies on the weekends.

What's an aphrodisiac of a curvy "Camelback"?
A hijacking, wisecracking, "slipcover" knick-knack.

A tuxedo "Loveseat" with a cushioned lap…
is where couples curl up for an afternoon nap.

For "Sectional" clients, I'm a "lounging" therapist…
Add a velvet ottoman for a sophisticated twist.

I'm laidback and low, my height is my might…
A comfy place to write. You'll sit at first sight.

Chapter 46   "A Writer's Recipe"

These are the ingredients that started my trip…
Family. Faith. Friends. Worship.

Roast beef after church, salmon croquettes after school…
Learned to cook Mustard greens with Neckbones as a rule.

Chitlins and Cornbread. Macaroni and cheese…
Brought in the New Year with Black-eyed peas.

Falling autumn leaves, Ox tails, red beans, and rice…
Enjoyed "Poi" at a Luau, with a pineapple slice.

A Tuna sandwich in my lunchbox, mom's love in each bite…
My High School classmate feasted on "Vegemite".

When I think of home, I think of Sweet Potato Pie…
S'mores at Summer camp, a Catfish Fry.

Chicken and Dumplings while hibernating…
Ice Cream churned on the porch, kin anxiously waiting.

I'm "Famous Amos" Cookies, an "Orange Julius" at the mall…
I'm Corn Dogs at the fair, peanuts, and baseball.

South Philly, the cheesesteak "Champs" of the East Coast…
Had "Scrapple" for breakfast with jellied toast.

"Cream of Wheat" or cold cereal, and my favorite spoon…
accompanied me watching Saturday cartoons.

Chocolate chip and Sugar Cookies were given as gifts…
Blessed that life's journey is moving swift.

My loving family tree is my writing recipe…
I'm **a Dreamer** in the authentic version of me.

Chapter 47   "Miss Rose A. Parks"

I'm a wooden work of art with "plot twisting" skill…
A "Red Carpet" moment in hunting goodwill.

For dogwalkers, tree-talkers, lawn mowing is key…
Breadcrumbs meant for ducks,
fed the pigeon that "clowned" me.

I'm a lamppost philosopher, an author of books…
I'm "Barefoot in the Park" despite the squirrels' funny looks.

I was a silent prop, in the film "Forrest Gump"…
as he captivated audiences sitting on his rump.

A resting place between workouts, like jogging or walking…
for handholding sweethearts, or sidewalk chalking.

For those grieving, commemorating, and nothing to hide…
I'm a whisper heard, on the other side.

Chapter 48   "Ferry Ride"

Perched atop the ferry's railing, for a scenic ride…
Vehicles cross the stern ramp, walk-ons sat inside.

A tourist in my hometown, sailing into the sunset…
Voyaging across Puget Sound, without luggage or ticket.

Three short horn blasts, a signal to rehearse…
Staying afloat, departing the dock in reverse.

White caps, choppy waves, up and down we go…
As we cruise along, sea lions steal the show.

"Port" is the Left side; "Starboard" is the right…
The "hull" is the body, like armor on knights.

Have seen Bremerton's Museum of the United States Navy…
Peeked in the galley, saw biscuits, and gravy.

For cafés and shopping, "Harborside Fountain Park"…
Saw Vashon, Bainbridge, and Whidbey Islands before dark.

After repairs and overhauling, vessels can navigate…
Witnessed a lifesaving moment from a brave shipmate.

Moving without wheels, passengers, and cargo…
had an experience with a ball of Alaskan snow.

Been to British Columbia, a feathered skinny-dipper…
"A day-tripper" with a skipper, lounged on "The Clipper".

Port Orchard is surrounded by **Evergreen trees**…
Alive-ing as I'm diving on fish if I please.

Inexpensive, reliable, "the" tugboat of the Northwest…
Whilst on board, I think I'll sit here and nest.

Chapter 49   "Radiohead"

"O Holy Night" was a song that made history…
Detective "Dick Tracy" solved comic strip mysteries.

"Jack Leroy Cooper", a patriarch of Vaudeville…
Promoted and performed with effortless skill.

Fun and folly with "Fibber McGee and Molly"…
Jolly slapstick from Stan Laurel and Ollie.

Heard "Orson Welles" narrating a "Martian invasion"…
and the "Blondie" serenade on occasion.

Wanted "Little Orphan Annie's" secret decoder ring…
Loved "Ozzie and Harriet" and the suspenders of "Larry King".

"Who's On First?", a sketch by "Abbott and Costello"…
"Burns and Allen" comedy. Shakespeare's "Othello".

American Graffiti and the "*howl*" of "Wolfman Jack"…
Records, cassette tapes, the infamous "8-track".

"Play Misty for Me", is a thrilling screenplay…
Tuned in. Turnt up, with something to say.

Cincinnati broadcasted a fictional radio station…
Ladies love a "Badd" rapper and his Kangol presentation.

My secret "Krush" is my boombox. I'm a Radiohead…
Counting sheep, helps me sleep, as they jump over my bed.

Chapter 50   The "Good-bye" Girl

I'm *outta'* here "Bro".
Where are my car keys?
I'm allergic to apologies on insincere knees.

The phone calls. The love letters, pleading profoundly…
Your circus performances "clowning around-ly".

Quite honestly "homie" I really don't care…
Truth in my composure,
I'm trying *not* to swear.

Jilted. Guilted, then *tilted*. I hadn't seen "**me**" in years…
Bye-Bye, stay "Fly" shedding crocodile tears.

We haven't been "us" for way too long…
So, I'm doing the "ghosting" as my "Exit" song.

Chapter 51 "Basket case"

> I'm storage for stuff. I make a lovely fruit bowl…
> I'm an adorable toy chest for clutter control.
>
> Spring has sprung, as bunnies embark…
> With red gingham napkins for lunch at the park.
>
> As a muse of art and cultural traditions…
> I'm the legacy of ancestors, making décor decisions.
>
> I'm a bookworm who adores showcasing flowers…
> I can stash extra cash. I can sit for hours.
>
> My woven woody-ness is the reason for my vanity…
> I'm a "basket case", which explains my insanity.

Chapter 52 "Fan Club"

My propelling is compelling, I'm popular that way…
A ceiling aficionado on a hot day.

I'm a rotating arrangement, an assembly of blades…
Wood, plastic, and metal are my masquerades.

Turning and telling, lazily slowing…
Whipping and stirring. Oscillating, and flowing.

I'm a *breezy* fan-atic with quiet chatter…
Spinning endlessly with a soft "pitter-patter".

Plugged in, snugged in, feeling just fine…
I exude enthusiasm and divine design.

Chapter 53   The "Bourgeois" Belt

I accentuate the waist giving trousers hope…
Made from leather, canvas, vinyl, or rope.

A "style" snob doing my job of tucking-in shirts…
Blue jeans "bestie", as well as shorts and skirts.

If suspenders surrender, I giggle and chuckle…
I hold up garments and adorn with a buckle.

I'm utilitarian carrying objects like tools…
I'm a guitar strap or jewelry. There are no rules.

For students who master their Martial Arts training…
For wrestlers and boxers and the title they're obtaining.

I keep the timing for harmonizing automobiles…
I'm a key fob for motorcycles with two or three wheels.

Looping the waist, a tailored length…
Upholding loyalty with unbreakable strength.

Chapter 54   "Captain Cleo Von Kraken"

A King-fin among Sharks, while swimming I pause…
Did you know I had a cameo in the movie "Jaws"?

Some Lobsters are mobsters towards Salmon and Shrimp…
Mi Familia? Starfishes. Octopus love to "pimp".

There's no doubt Rainbow Trout are sea gypsies with clout…
A Mermaid made a splash at a New York hangout.

When Dolphins squawk, what do they say?
Do they ask Whales and Sea Turtles if they want to play?

Galloping with Seahorses, while swimming I pause…
Did you see my performance in the blockbuster, "Jaws"?

Marlins are darlin', a highly prized game…
River Carp stay sharp cultivating their fame.

Bass are classy and sassy, the So-fish-ticated type…
There's a fish known as "Wanda", believe the hype.

I'm "chill" by the windowsill, teasing cats for a thrill…
Sudden spills, water bills and daily refills.

Cruising like a Barracuda, while swimming I pause…
I did my own stunts for a summer thriller called "Jaws".

Took a voyage to Atlantis, researched Yellow Perch…
Slow-moving rivers are where they like to lurch.

Met Tuna Turner, Nat King Cod, Meryl Stream…
Befriended Mr. Limpet and James Pond in a dream.

In a fishbowl dwelling, but a 'Tiger of the Sea'…
"Captain Cleo Von Kraken", the name given to me.

Like Hemingway at a Stingray café, I pause…
Did I mention I was Oscar-nominated for the film "Jaws"?

Chapter 55   "Aesthetic"

Do not knock my hustle. Do not mock my fame...
Creative. Unique. "Aesthetic" is my name.

Bossed Up. Flossed Up. Love and Mercy...
I'm a designer handbag, feeling purse-ee.

I'm Art. I'm Architecture. I'm soulful expression...
I'm objects appreciated. I'm a humanity lesson.

I'm "hot" as fish grease, or a Jalapeno's armpit...
Reinventing iconic. No lie, I'm true grit.

Did you know I'm "All This"?
Did you know I'm "All That"?
Did you know I'm the one whose philosophically "Phat"?

I'm a remarkable criminal, stealing the show...
My overall style gave rhythm its flow.

From the depths of perception and its theory...
I'm the experience of charming and the beauty of eerie.

Dramatic, Epic, Tony-winning plays...
The heartbeat of music and its lyrical ways.

I'm a set of principles guiding a movement...
I'm a "feel good" mood, with room for improvement.

Filled with emotion, a love potion promotion...
I'm a locomotion commotion. Devotion's the notion.

Uplifting the senses, I'm the essence of cute...
Charming. Inventive. Elegance in pursuit.

I'm Widgets, and gadgets, and "thing-a-ma-bobs"...
"Quirky" and I have similar jobs.

Do not knock my hustle. Do not mock my fame...
Creative. Unique. "Aesthetic" is my name.

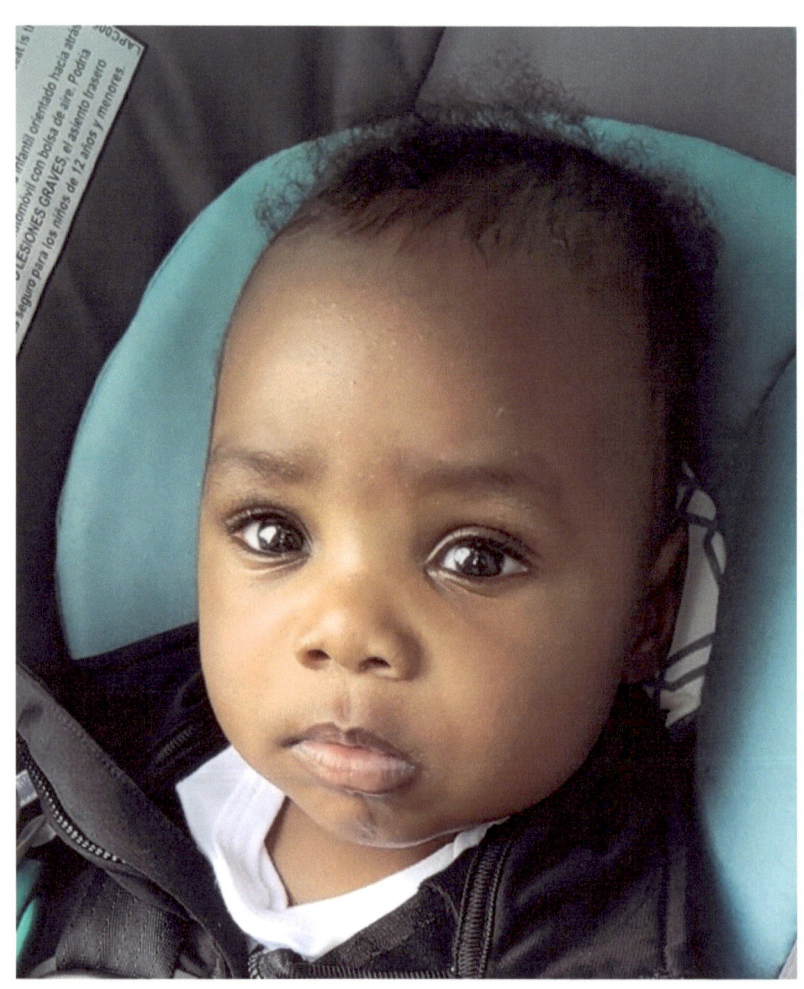

Chapter 56 "Bryson Rashad Nickles"

He's **B**rilliant, Mind-**B**oggling, & cannot **B**e ignored…
Listening to "**B**eethoven" whenever he's **B**ored.

A **B**ig Shot among **B**illionaires, or **B**ears at the Zoo…
He **B**oomerangs when **B**usy, like **B**umble **B**ees do.

Some say that his **B**utler, **B**orn in **B**oston, named "Dallas"…
served **B**ritain's Royal Family at **B**uckingham Palace.

He's **B**ananas & **B**utterscotch. He'll give you the Grins…
Hitting homeruns in **B**aseball were everyone Wins.

Has earned **B**adges in **B**ravery. He's Cool & **B**reezy…
Charming as Seven Dwarfs, minus Grumpy & Sneezy.

Behind a **B**rick **B**uilding, **B**ad Guys ran out of Luck…
He **B**usted the **B**andits, trying to steal a Truck.

He put the **B**ackspin in **B**owling. Earned a master's degree…
as "The **B**ook-reading **B**andit", no one's Nicer than he.

Never **B**luffs playing **B**ackgammon, in the **B**link of an eye…
He's a **B**eliever. A Dreamer. He's **B**lueberry Pie.

He **B**reaks down **B**arriers, from Shakespeare he Quotes…
A **B**asketball **B**uzzer **B**eater. He's music notes.

He's **B**rilliant, Mind-**B**oggling, my Heart he tickles…
He's a **B**lessing. He's my cousin, "**B**ryson Rashad Nickles".

Acknowledgements

*A warm-hearted Thank you to all of the people
who inspired and helped me through the process of
finishing this book.
This project would not be possible
without the support of many people.*

**Author, Mr. John A. Huguley
Book Publishing & Literary Services Consultant**

The chance encounter that changed my life.
Thank you, Mr. Huguley,
no one has been more encouraging or
supportive on this journey.
This book wouldn't have been completed
without your expertise and tutelage.

Please pick up a copy of his book,
"Diamonds, Dollars, and Roses" available on Amazon
Official website: www.johnhuguley.com

**Pencil & Watercolor Illustrations by
Mr. Dan Flood**

**Photography Images by
Pexels**

Special Thanks to:

In Alphabetical order by First Name:

Adidas (Apparel & Footwear)
Auburn Valley Creative Arts Gallery
Ms. Candace Luckett (The Mane Blueprint Hair Salon)
Everlast Sports Equipment
Graco Baby
Mr. & Mrs. Rashad Nickles
Titleist Golf Equipment
Treehouse Point (Issaquah, WA)
Washington State Ferries (WSDOT)

Thank you to the Extraordinary Proofreading, Creative Consulting, and Editing Team

In Alphabetical order by First Name:

Ms. Ann R. DeWitty
Mrs. Charlotte Nickles
Mr. Dan Flood
Ms. Danielle Richard
Mr. Darryl Coker
Mr. James Kuebler
Mr. John A. Huguley

(Hair Styled by Ms. Candace Luckett of "The Mane Blueprint" Hair Salon)

About the Author

    Published Author Charron M. Mollette of the books "Pen and Paper", "Granny's Camera", and "Coffee On Tuesday", is a native of Seattle, Washington. Her previous work was included in the book "Under the Harvest Moon" where she received the "Editor's Choice Award" from the National Library of Poetry. A huge fan of Shel Silverstein, Shakespeare, and Robert Frost, she also enjoys Art Galleries and Museums.

www.ingramcontent.com/pod-product-compliance
Lightning Source LLC
Chambersburg PA
CBHW042308150426
43198CB00001B/7